"NO PRISONER IS SEEN BY ANOTHER, AFTER HE ENTERS THE WALL. WHEN THE YEARS OF HIS CONFINEMENT HAVE PASSED, HIS OLD ASSOCIATES IN CRIME WILL BE SCATTERED OVER THE EARTH, OR IN THE GRAVE...AND THE PRISONER CAN GO FORTH INTO A NEW AND INDUSTRIOUS LIFE, WHERE HIS PREVIOUS MISDEEDS ARE UNKNOWN."

FROM THE FIRST AND SECOND ANNUAL REPORTS
OF THE INSPECTORS OF THE EASTERN STATE PENITENTIARY
(PHILADELPHIA 1831)

LIFE IN PRISON

PHILADELPHIA, 21 OCTOBER 1994
I'M IN PHILLY TO TOUR EASTERN STATE PENITENTIARY. FOR A DEFUNCT VICTORIAN PRISON, IT DOESN'T LOOK SO BAD.
HI JULIE. HI TODD.
WELCOME TO EASTERN STATE, CHRIS. HERE, YOU'LL NEED TO WEAR THIS HARD HAT. THIS PLACE IS FALLING APART AT THE SEAMS.
CREEEEK
COME ON IN! HOW WAS YOUR TRIP?
THIS IS JULIE COURTNEY AND TODD GILENS. THEY ARE THE CURATORS WHO INVITED ME TO COME DOWN TO EASTERN STATE TO HAVE A LOOK AROUND.
I MADE GOOD TIME.
EACH ARTIST WILL USE DIFFERENT PARTS OF THE PRISON FOR THEIR INSTALLATIONS
SO, DOWN TO BUSINESS. 12 ARTISTS, INCLUDING YOU AND SIMON - IF YOU CAN COME UP WITH AN IDEA, WILL MAKE NEW ARTWORKS INSIDE THE PRISON IN MAY.
YOU SHOULD HAVE A LOOK AROUND THE PLACE.
FEEL FREE TO EXPLORE. I HOPE YOU CAN COME UP WITH AN IDEA FOR THIS SHOW.
TO START WITH, I'D LIKE TO GO UP THAT CENTRAL TOWER AND HAVE A LOOK.

SIMON, I HAVE MY VIDEO CAMERA AND TRIPOD, SO I'LL TAPE PART OF MY TOUR OF THE PRISON - I'LL UPLOAD SOME OF THESE SHOTS TO YOU ONCE I GET BACK TO THE TRAIN. AS I'M WALKING AROUND, I'M STRUCK BY THE SIMILARITIES BETWEEN THIS PLACE AND STRANGEWAYS.

THIS PLACE IS SO FUCKING OPPRESSIVE. HOW COULD ANYONE SURVIVE LIVING HERE?

Prison #1

IT SAYS IN THE BROCHURE THAT WHEN THIS PLACE WAS BUILT, THE PRISONERS WERE ISOLATED IN THEIR CELLS 24 HOURS A DAY. EACH CELL WAS SELF-CONTAINED WITH IT'S OWN TOILET AND EXERCISE YARD. THE VICTORIAN IDEA WAS TO ELIMINATE THE CORRUPTING INFLUENCE OF OTHER PRISONERS BY SEALING PEOPLE AWAY FOR THE DURATION OF INTERNMENT.

I'LL CALL YOU THE MINUTE I GET BACK TO NEW YORK. I THINK WE CAN USE ONE OF OUR EXISTING IDEAS FOR THE SHOW HERE.

HEY! I'M JUST BACK FROM PHILLY. THEY'D LIKE TO COMMISSION A NEW ARTWORK. THIS WOULD BE A GOOD TIME TO DO THAT COMIC BOOK IDEA WE HAD.
PLONK
SSST...
WE COULD MAKE A COMIC BOOK ABOUT PRISON LIFE, BUT THERE'S JUST ONE PROBLEM. NEITHER OF US HAS DONE TIME.
WELL, MY BROTHER DID 30 DAYS IN THE COUNTY JAIL. WE COULD TALK TO HIM...
...SST...
OF COURSE! SEAN KEATING IS A MATE OF MINE AND HE'S DONE TIME. I'VE ALSO GOT GOOD CONNECTIONS AT STRANGEWAYS PRISON HERE IN MANCHESTER. AFTER ALL, I DID HELP THEM START A VISITING ARTIST PROGRAM.
SLURP...
FAB! WE ARE AWAY. A 28 PAGE COMIC IS NOT MUCH ROOM. GIVE ME A CALL AFTER YOU TALK TO SEAN.
SO, IN A NUT SHELL, THAT'S THE LIFE IN PRISON ORIGIN STORY. AND NOW, FOR THE REAL THING...

THE STEEL DOOR

SEAN KEATING

WELL, AS EARLY AS I CAN REMEMBER, I ALWAYS WANTED TO BE A GANGSTER. I SUPPOSE IT'S MY DAD'S FAULT REALLY. HE USED TO SAY 'WATCH THIS FILM, IT'S AN ACE FILM!' EDWARD G. ROBINSON, JIMMY CAGNEY, YOU KNOW WHAT I MEAN...

TOP OF THE WORLD!

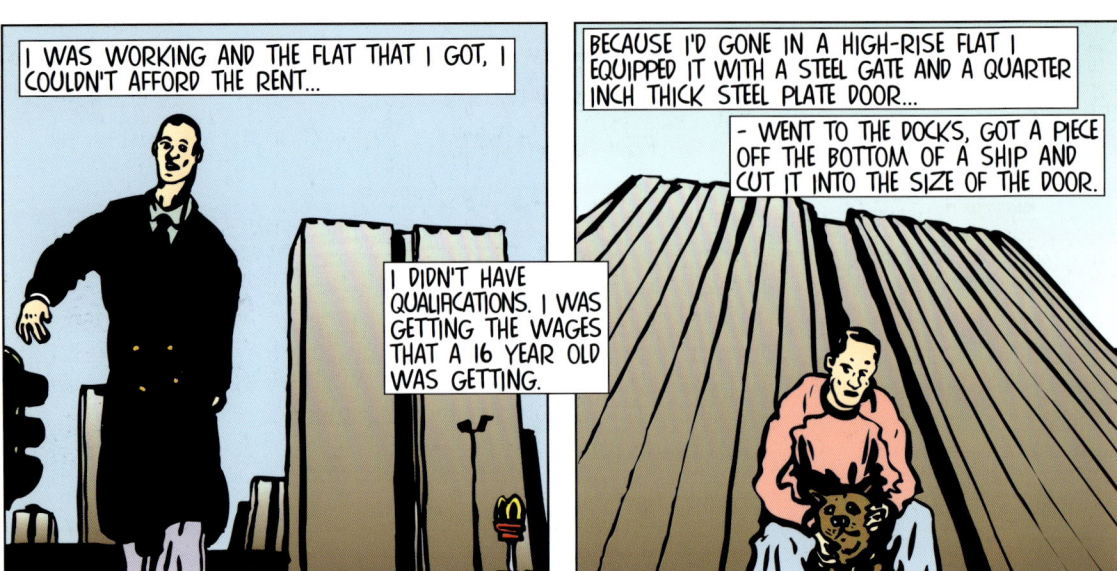

I WAS WORKING AND THE FLAT THAT I GOT, I COULDN'T AFFORD THE RENT...

BECAUSE I'D GONE IN A HIGH-RISE FLAT I EQUIPPED IT WITH A STEEL GATE AND A QUARTER INCH THICK STEEL PLATE DOOR...

- WENT TO THE DOCKS, GOT A PIECE OFF THE BOTTOM OF A SHIP AND CUT IT INTO THE SIZE OF THE DOOR.

I DIDN'T HAVE QUALIFICATIONS. I WAS GETTING THE WAGES THAT A 16 YEAR OLD WAS GETTING.

AND IT WAS POINTED OUT TO ME THAT IF I HAD THE EQUIPMENT THERE TO DELAY THE POLICE, WHY NOT BECOME A DRUG DEALER.

SO WHY THE FUCK NOT?

I'M WORKING IN THIS CLOTHES SHOP, ASPECTO CLOTHING, AND I SAID TO THIS GUY --

I'VE BEEN HERE 3 MONTHS, AND I'M SELLING LIKE PAUL SMITH SUITS AND KATHERINE HAMNETT GEAR TO STUDIO EXECUTIVES, WELL WHERE'S MY COMMISSION? I'M ONLY ON 70 ODD A WEEK.

THERE'S NO MONEY.

SO I STARTED SELLING IT TO MY MATES AND THAT, AND BEFORE LONG THE DOOR NEVER STOPPED.

IT WAS THE MATTE BLACK DREAM HOUSE, BUT RIGHT IN THE MIDDLE OF SALFORD PRECINCT.

I THOUGHT I'D MADE IT, YOU KNOW WHAT I MEAN, I'M TOP OF THE WORLD, WHICH TECHNICALLY I WAS BECAUSE I WAS FUCKING TEN STORIES HIGH UP.

IT WASN'T LONG BEFORE I BECAME KNOWN TO THE POLICE.

THERE'S ME AND ANOTHER FIVE DEALERS, WE WERE ALL PLAYING CARDS IN MY FLAT...

SOMETHING JUST DIDN'T FEEL RIGHT,
I JUST COULDN'T SETTLE, SO LIKE HALF AN HOUR LATER I GOES TO THE WINDOW...
I COULD SEE LIKE FUCKING BIG LONG SHADOWS, IT WAS LIKE SOMETHING OUT OF A SPAGHETTI WESTERN.
KNOCK
KNOCK
KNOCK
WHO IS IT?
WE'RE FROM THE COUNCIL, HAVE YOU GOT A DRAW*
LISTEN MATE, FIRST OF ALL I DON'T KNOW WHAT DRAW IS...
YOU KNOW WHEN YOU HEAR THINGS...
YOU'RE NOT SUPPOSED TO HEAR THEM BUT YOU DO,
BAM BAM BAM
I HEARD THIS STATIC FROM A RADIO...
TURN THE FUCKING MUSIC DOWN, CLEAR THE TABLE GET THE ASHTRAY, GET ALL THE ROACHES* OUT OF IT! SHIT!
SEAN KEATING OPEN YOUR DOOR!
OPEN MY DOOR? WHAT DO YOU WANT OFFICER?
OPEN YOUR FUCKING DOOR!

* MARIJUANA

BAM
BAM
BAM
I GRABBED LIKE FUCKING TWO AND A HALF OUNCES OF DRAW CUT UP, A SHEET OF ACID TABS, FIFTY ALL WRAPPED UP READY FOR SELLING, RIGHT, AND TWO GRAMMES OF COKE FOR MY OWN PERSONAL.
SO I GOT MY ARM AND RAMMED IT DOWN THE U-BEND IN THE TOILET...
FLUSHED THE TOILET AND RAN TO THE DOOR.
BAM
I DIDN'T KNOW WHETHER THE DOOR WOULD HOLD OUT OR NOT
THAT'S BANG ON TOP...
I LOOKED DOWN AT MY ARM... ALL ONE SIDE OF MY BODY WAS FUCKING WET FROM THE TOILET.
SO I THROWS THE SHIRT IN THE SINK.
BAM
BAM
BAM
EVERYONE'S RUNNING AROUND EATING DRUGS, STICKING DRUGS UP THEIR ARSE. WE'RE LIKE IRONING CLOTHES AND REALLY WEIRD THINGS LIKE, ALL LOOKING OUR BEST FOR COURT IN THE MORNING.
SO NEXT THING THE BANGING STOPPED...
OPEN THIS FUCKING DOOR!

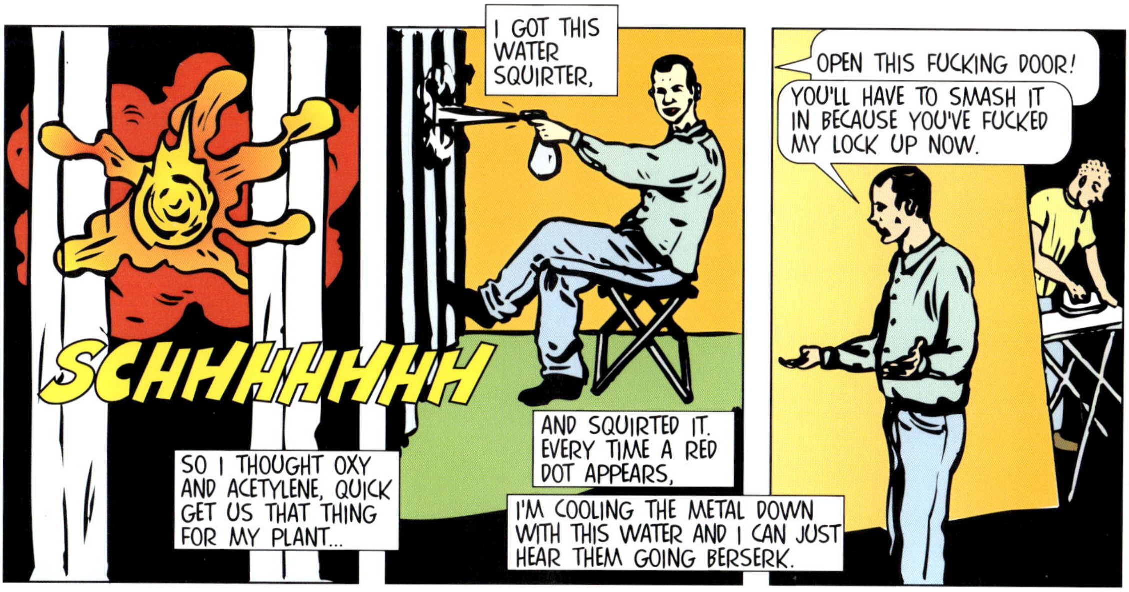

I HAD A NEW HUGO BOSS CASHMERE BLAZER ON, LINEN SLACKS WITH SILK LINING AND ALL OF THAT, THESE SHOES, MY HAIR ALL SLICKED BACK, GEORGINA VENEZDORF HAND PRINTED TIE, GOLD CUFFLINKS AND ALL THAT. I THOUGHT I WAS THE BEES KNEES STOOD THERE.

I'LL NEVER FORGET HIS NAME. JUDGE KERSHAW HE WAS CALLED. A RIGHT BASTARD. HE JUST LOOKED OVER HIS GLASSES AT ME AND WENT...

"I CAN'T SEE ANY REASON WHY THIS MAN SHOULDN'T GO TO PRISON. HE'S SOLD DRUGS."

I'M THERE LIKE, NINE OF US IN THIS FUCKING ROOM ABOUT SIX FOOT WIDE AND SIX FOOT LONG...

WITH BIG THICK PLASTIC GLASS AT THE BACK WHERE IT HAD ALL BEEN SCRATCHED AND THAT, HAD SHIT THROWN UP IT AND ALL. IT HAD A LIGHT BULB BEHIND IT, IT WAS LIKE SOMETHING OUT OF THE DARK AGES.

YOU THOUGHT YOU WERE GOING OUT AND ALL THAT, DIDN'T YOU?

SO APPROACHING THESE DOUBLE GATES, I'M THINKING YEAH TOP OF THE WORLD, AND THEN IT HIT, HOW CAN IT BE TOP OF THE WORLD, YOU'RE IN JAIL. IT'S NOT LIKE IN FILMS WHERE YEARS CAN BE COVERED IN THE SPACE OF NINETY MINUTES. I WASN'T THERE FOR NINETY MINUTES. IT WAS JUST FUCKING SO DEPRESSING.

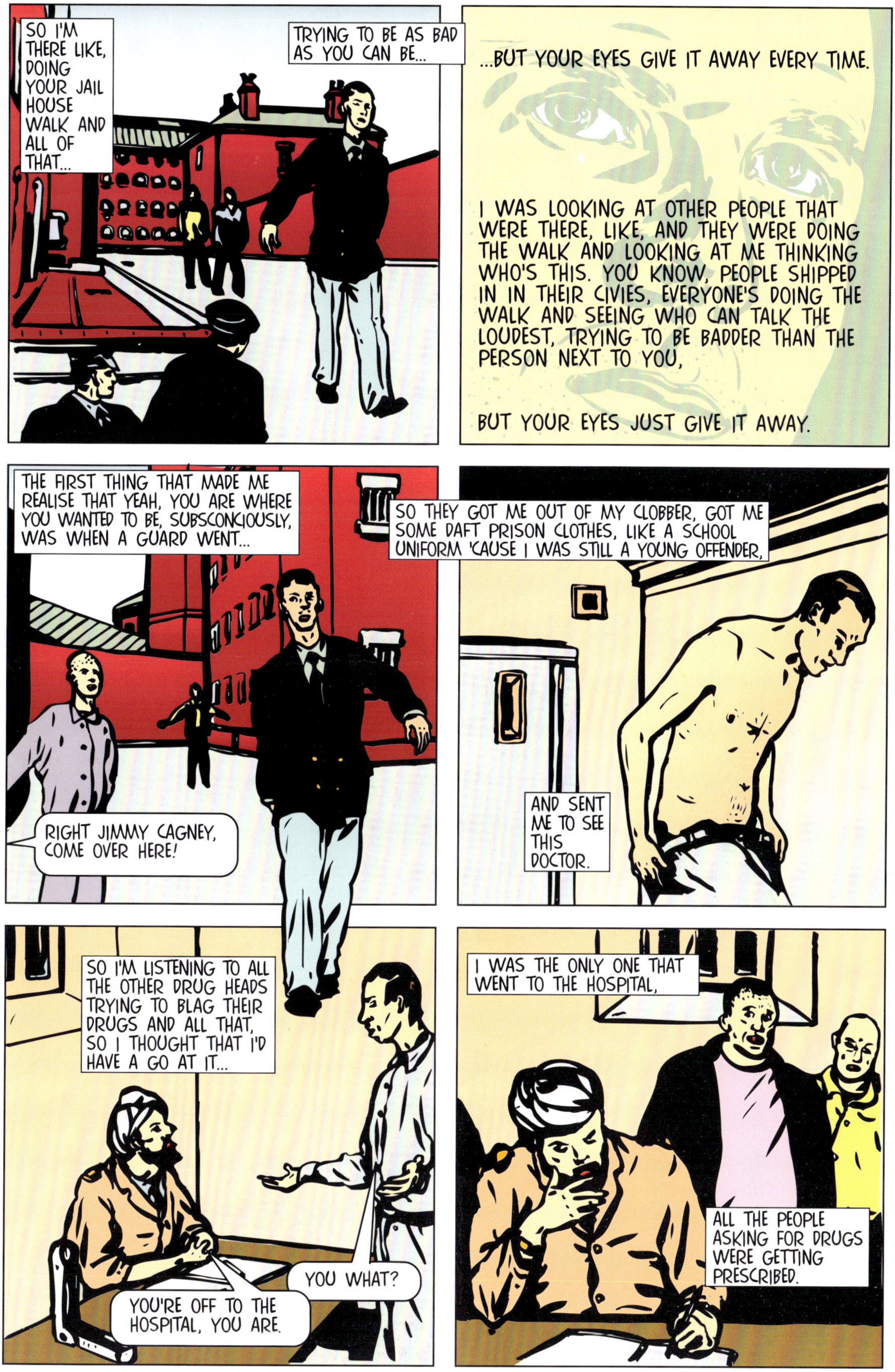
SO I'M THERE LIKE, DOING YOUR JAIL HOUSE WALK AND ALL OF THAT...
TRYING TO BE AS BAD AS YOU CAN BE...
...BUT YOUR EYES GIVE IT AWAY EVERY TIME.
I WAS LOOKING AT OTHER PEOPLE THAT WERE THERE, LIKE, AND THEY WERE DOING THE WALK AND LOOKING AT ME THINKING WHO'S THIS. YOU KNOW, PEOPLE SHIPPED IN IN THEIR CIVIES, EVERYONE'S DOING THE WALK AND SEEING WHO CAN TALK THE LOUDEST, TRYING TO BE BADDER THAN THE PERSON NEXT TO YOU,
BUT YOUR EYES JUST GIVE IT AWAY.
THE FIRST THING THAT MADE ME REALISE THAT YEAH, YOU ARE WHERE YOU WANTED TO BE, SUBSCONCIOUSLY, WAS WHEN A GUARD WENT...
RIGHT JIMMY CAGNEY, COME OVER HERE!
SO THEY GOT ME OUT OF MY CLOBBER, GOT ME SOME DAFT PRISON CLOTHES, LIKE A SCHOOL UNIFORM 'CAUSE I WAS STILL A YOUNG OFFENDER,
AND SENT ME TO SEE THIS DOCTOR.
SO I'M LISTENING TO ALL THE OTHER DRUG HEADS TRYING TO BLAG THEIR DRUGS AND ALL THAT, SO I THOUGHT THAT I'D HAVE A GO AT IT...
YOU'RE OFF TO THE HOSPITAL, YOU ARE.
YOU WHAT?
I WAS THE ONLY ONE THAT WENT TO THE HOSPITAL,
ALL THE PEOPLE ASKING FOR DRUGS WERE GETTING PRESCRIBED.

SO I'M GOING DOWN THIS CORRIDOR - THIS WAS ABOUT EIGHT O'CLOCK AT NIGHT - DOWN THIS CORRIDOR ITS LIKE DIM LIGHTS. FLOORS IMMACULATE, ALL THE WALLS ARE BRILLIANT WHITE AND ALL.

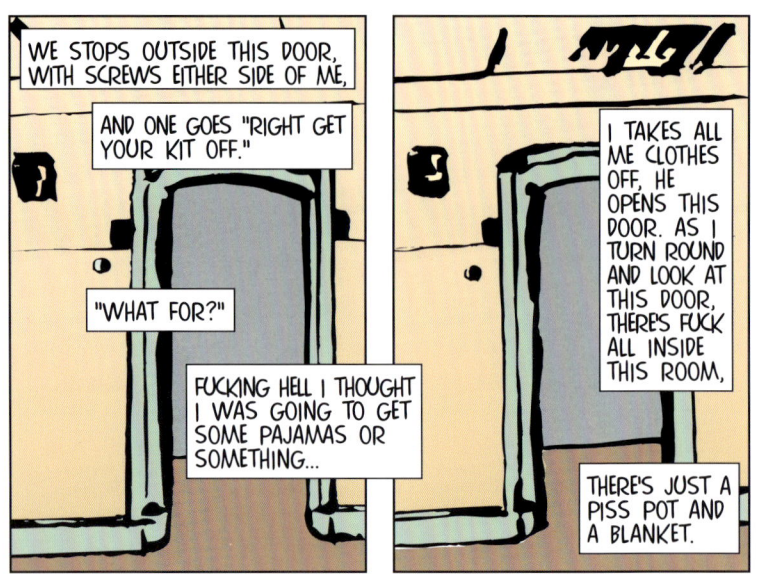

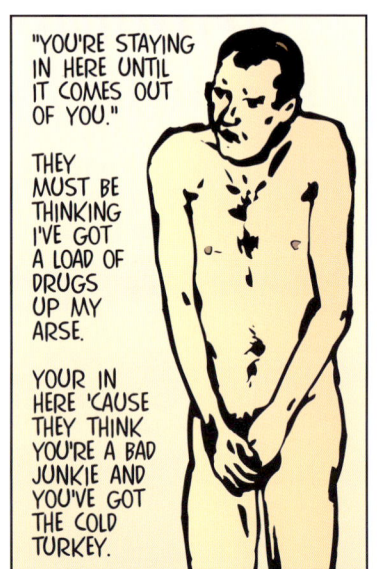

WE STOPS OUTSIDE THIS DOOR, WITH SCREWS EITHER SIDE OF ME,

AND ONE GOES "RIGHT GET YOUR KIT OFF."

"WHAT FOR?"

FUCKING HELL I THOUGHT I WAS GOING TO GET SOME PAJAMAS OR SOMETHING...

I TAKES ALL ME CLOTHES OFF, HE OPENS THIS DOOR. AS I TURN ROUND AND LOOK AT THIS DOOR, THERE'S FUCK ALL INSIDE THIS ROOM,

THERE'S JUST A PISS POT AND A BLANKET.

SO I SORT OF TURN, AND AS I LOOK BACK AT HIM HE JUST GOES...

...AND FUCKING SHOVES ME IN THIS ROOM, ON THIS SLIPPY FLOOR ON MY ARSE.

IN!

"YOU'RE STAYING IN HERE UNTIL IT COMES OUT OF YOU."

THEY MUST BE THINKING I'VE GOT A LOAD OF DRUGS UP MY ARSE.

YOUR IN HERE 'CAUSE THEY THINK YOU'RE A BAD JUNKIE AND YOU'VE GOT THE COLD TURKEY.

SO I'M JUST HUDDLED IN THE CORNER WITH THIS BLANKET ROUND ME.

WITH IT BEING A STRIP CELL, PEOPLE HAD SHIT UP THE WALLS AS THEIR WAY OF ATTACKING THE SYSTEM.

SO IT WAS FUCKING HANGING.

SO I LOOKED AT THIS TILE, AND MY DAD'S FACE WAS ON THIS TILE.

IT WASN'T JUST MY DAD'S FACE, IT WAS LIKE MY DAD'S HEAD WITH HIS BEARD AND HIS HAIR.

THIS WAS FUCKING HEAVY. WHATEVER ANGLE I LOOKED AT IT FROM IT WAS THERE, HIS PIERCING EYES, LOOKING RIGHT AT ME.

IT WAS KIND OF LIKE REASSURING, 'CAUSE IT WAS MY FIRST NIGHT IN PRISON.

IT SEEMED LIKE AGES, BUT IT PROBABLY WASN'T, AN HOUR OR SO, I FELL ASLEEP.

RIGHT, EMPTY YOUR PISS POT.
THERE'S LOADS OF OTHER NAKED MALES WALKING ABOUT. EVERYONE'S DOING THE JAIL HOUSE WALK,
BUT WITH NO CLOTHES ON, THEIR BALLS ARE FUCKING GOING EVERYWHERE.
I'M NOT A STOCKY KIND OF PERSON.
LOOK AT THAT FUCKING SKINNY BASTARD
I SAW THIS GUARD AND EXPLAINED THE SITUATION, NOT THAT I WAS TRYING TO BLAG DRUGS, JUST THAT THE DOCTOR HAD MISUNDERSTOOD.
SO I GETS PUT BACK ON THE WING IN A SINGLE CELL.
I WAS SCARED THAT I WAS GOING TO GET CUT OR HAVE SOME BIG FUCKER SHAGGING MY ARSE.
I'LL TELL YOU WHAT ELSE WAS WEIRD, RIGHT,
I WAS DEVISING WAYS OF STEALING THE PRISON GEAR AS A SOUVENIR, FOR WHEN I GOT OUT.
MY SECOND NIGHT THEY PUTS THIS FUCKING LUNATIC IN WITH ME,
ALL YOU CAN GET OUT OF HIM IS CARS, HOW TO ROB THEM.
I TOLD HIM NOT TO PISS IN THE POT.
THIS IS MY CELL, IT'S MY HOME NOW, AND I DON'T WANT YOU DOING THAT IN HERE.
ANYWAY, I'M LOOKING AT ALL HIS CAR PICTURES ON THE WALL AND THINKING, I CAN'T BE DOING WITH THIS IN HERE WITH ME TWENTY THREE HOURS A DAY.
SO I RIPPED ALL HIS PICTURES OFF THE WALL.
LITTLE BASTARD.
I ROLLED EVERYTHING UP INTO HIS MATTRESS...

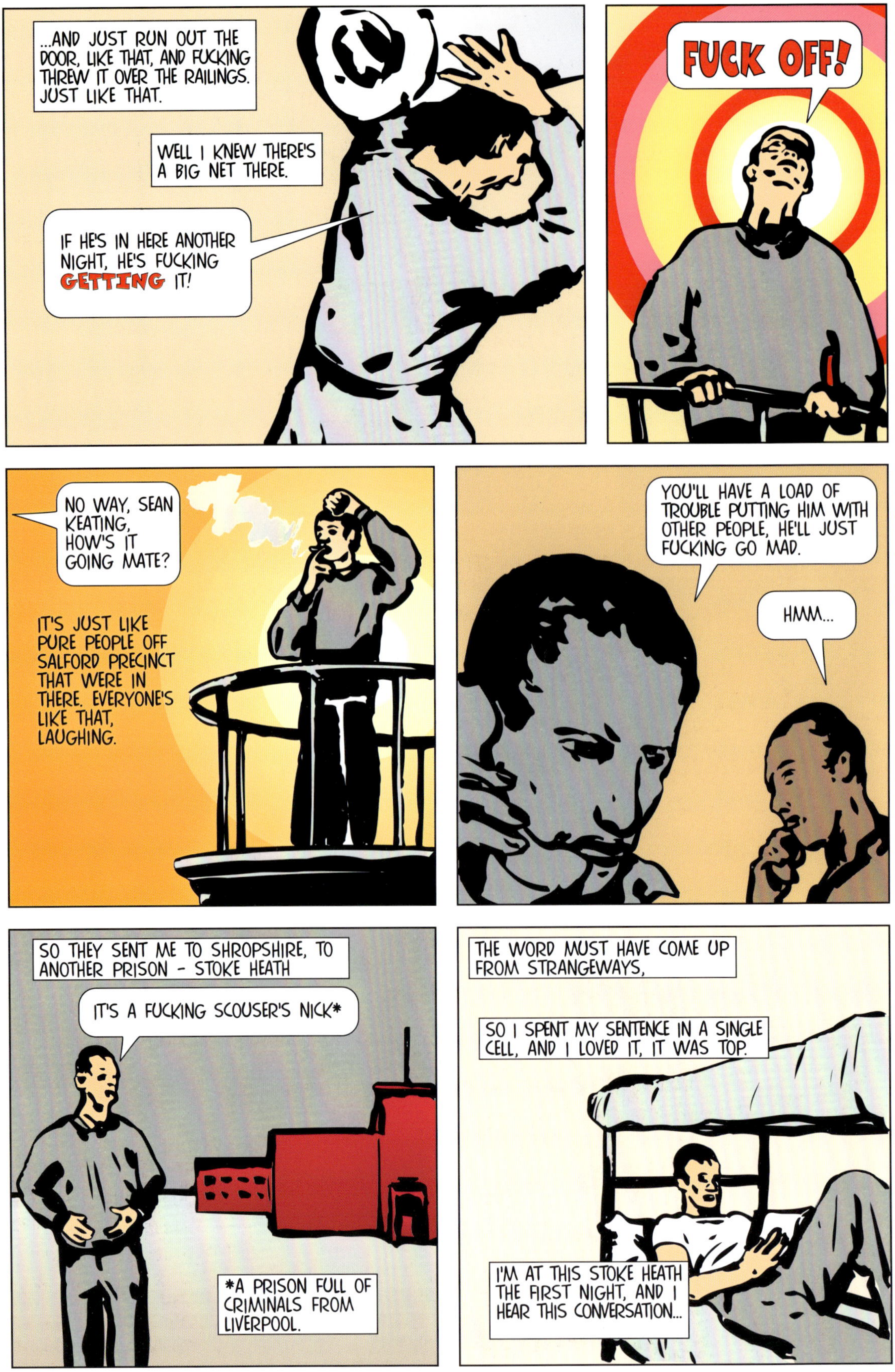
...AND JUST RUN OUT THE DOOR, LIKE THAT, AND FUCKING THREW IT OVER THE RAILINGS. JUST LIKE THAT.
WELL I KNEW THERE'S A BIG NET THERE.
IF HE'S IN HERE ANOTHER NIGHT, HE'S FUCKING GETTING IT!
FUCK OFF!
NO WAY, SEAN KEATING, HOW'S IT GOING MATE?
IT'S JUST LIKE PURE PEOPLE OFF SALFORD PRECINCT THAT WERE IN THERE. EVERYONE'S LIKE THAT, LAUGHING.
YOU'LL HAVE A LOAD OF TROUBLE PUTTING HIM WITH OTHER PEOPLE, HE'LL JUST FUCKING GO MAD.
HMM...
SO THEY SENT ME TO SHROPSHIRE, TO ANOTHER PRISON - STOKE HEATH
IT'S A FUCKING SCOUSER'S NICK*
*A PRISON FULL OF CRIMINALS FROM LIVERPOOL.
THE WORD MUST HAVE COME UP FROM STRANGEWAYS,
SO I SPENT MY SENTENCE IN A SINGLE CELL, AND I LOVED IT, IT WAS TOP.
I'M AT THIS STOKE HEATH THE FIRST NIGHT, AND I HEAR THIS CONVERSATION...

Panel 1: ...SO IF YOU LOOK IN THE BIBLE...

...DON'T GIVE ME THAT, MAN...

Panel 2: JESUS WAS A BLACK MAN.

Panel 3: WHAT DO YOU MEAN JESUS WAS A BLACK MAN!

Panel 4: WELL, IF YOU WENT TO SPAIN FOR TWO WEEKS YOU WOULDN'T COME BACK WHITE WOULD YOU, SO IMAGINE BEING BORN IN NAZARETH.

IF YOU'RE SAYING THAT JESUS WAS WHITE, THEN YOU MEAN THAT MOSES MUST HAVE LOOKED LIKE CHARLTON HESTON!

Panel 5: AT WHICH POINT THE GUY WHO'D BEEN ARGUING THE POINT STARTED PISSING HIMSELF LAUGHING.

SO THE NEXT MORNING, WHEN THE CELLS WERE OPEN, MY DOOR'S UNLOCKED LIKE, AND I'M JUST LAID THERE...

HEY!
YOU'RE WHITE!
WHAT OF IT?
JUST BECAUSE I'M WHITE DOESN'T CHANGE MY POINT.
HA HA HA HA HA HA
SO FROM THEN ON IN I GOT INTRODUCED TO THE BLACK CROWD. THESE BLACK LADS WERE FROM MOSS SIDE, THEY WERE SERIOUS.
IT WAS UNKNOWN TO ME, WHAT THEY WERE INTO, UNTIL I GOT OUT.
ALL THESE LADS I WAS GIVING LIP TO, SPARRING WITH AND HANGING OUT WITH...
FUCK!
MR. BIG REVEALED
THEY WERE HEAVYWEIGHT GANGSTERS. IT FUCKING FREAKED ME OUT! IN NO UNCERTAIN TERMS, THAT'S WHAT THEY WAS, GANGSTERS.
END

JAIL?, OH, HELL YES, I'VE BEEN THERE. NOT THE BIG HOUSE MIND YOU; I'M TALKING ABOUT THE CROWBAR HOTEL, THE HOOSKOW, THE COUNTY LOCKUP.

THE NIGHT I WAS BROUGHT IN, THE TRUSTEE TREATED ME TO A BEATING SO SEVERE I WAS TAKEN TO THE HOSPITAL. HAD I STAYED THE NIGHT IN THE LOCKUP I WOULD HAVE WOKE UP DEAD.

THE PRICE

MARK SPERANDIO

A REAL CON WILL TELL YOU THAT COUNTY TIME IS THE WORST TIME...

DOPE IS SCARCE AND UNRELIABLE, SEX IS A SOLITARY SPORT, AND YOU NEVER KNOW WHO YOUR NEIGHBORS ARE FROM DAY TO DAY...

WIFE BEATERS AND WINOS MIX FREELY WITH LITTERBUGS AND FORGERS, WHO SLEEP NEXT TO GIRLFRIEND STABBERS WHO PLAY CARDS WITH DUI'S AND BURGLARS...

ALMOST TO A MAN, WE WERE HERE FOR LOSING CONTROL OF OUR LIBIDOS AND INHIBITIONS WHILE UNDER THE INFLUENCE OF ALCOHOL.

I ENDED UP A GUEST OF THE COUNTY SHERIFF AFTER A PARTICULARLY SAVAGE BOUT OF DRINKING JUST PRIOR TO ATTENDING A FIREHALL VALENTINES DAY DANCE...

I HAD CONSUMED THE LIONS SHARE OF A LITER OF 151 RUM...
I DON'T REMEMBER A THING ABOUT THE DANCE...
IT HAS ALL BEEN RELATED TO ME THROUGH ANECDOTES.
THE SHERIFFS BOYS ARRIVED...
LED BY DEPUTY HARRISON.
HE APPROACHED FROM BEHIND...
MISTAKE.
MY LIZARD BRAIN WAS IN CHARGE WHILE I WAS AWAY...
MY GLANCING BLOW TO DEPUTY HARRISON'S THROAT...
...SUCCEEDED ONLY IN RIPPING OFF HIS WHISTLE, WHICH BECAME A TOY FOR THE OTHER DANCE-GOERS.
DOWN TO THE CONCRETE FLOOR I WENT AND OUT WENT THE REST OF THE LAST OF WHATEVER LIGHTS WAS IN MY BRAIN.
DEPUTY HARRISON INSISTED I PULL A FULL YEAR FOR THE EMBARRASSMENT HE SUFFERED...
BUT THE SEVERITY OF MY INJURIES AT THEIR HANDS WEIGHED HEAVILY IN MY FAVOR.
SO, WITH NO TRIAL OR FURTHER FANFARE, I AGREED TO SERVE 30 DAYS FOR PUBLIC INTOXICATION.

EVERY DAY THE SHERIFF (WHO WAS A KINDLY OLDER MAN WHO LIKED ME ANYHOW) WOULD RELEASE ME IN THE MORNING FOR DRUG COUNSELING TWO BLOCKS AWAY...
I WALKED THERE ON MY OWN, AND IN THE AFTERNOONS...
I SPENT MY TIME IN THE LOCAL LIBRARY...
The Gulag Archipelago
UPON MY RETURN IN THE LATE AFTERNOON, DEPUTY HARRISON WOULD BE WAITING TO FLEX HIS AUTHORITY.
HE WOULD HAVE LOVED TO HAVE CAUGHT ME BRINGING IN SOME SORT OF CONTRABAND...
SO I COULD SPEND MORE TIME UNDER HIS CONTROL.
NOBODY IS IN THE COUNTY STIR MORE THAN A YEAR. THAT WOULD BE CONSIDERED CRUEL AND UNUSUAL PUNISHMENT.
I PASSED MY TIME PEACEFULLY, SOBERLY AND PRIVATELY.
A PLASTIC BOTTLE FILLED WITH GRAIN ALCOHOL WOULD OCCASIONALLY FIND ITS WAY IN THROUGH THE CRACKS...
BUT I STAYED AWAY FROM IT AND ALL DRUGS WHILE I WAS THERE.

I READ ALL THE PRISON NOVELS IN THE STACKS OF THE LIBRARY. THE GULAG ARCHIPELAGO, PAPILLON, AND POW NONFICTION SUSTAINED ME...

THE NIGHTMARE OF REAL CONFINEMENT WITH NO HOPE OF RELEASE PUT MY SMALL PENITENCE IN PERSPECTIVE.

I SURVIVED THE MOST HUMILIATING EXPERIENCE OF MY LIFE RELATIVELY INTACT...

AND WALKED HOME ALONE SATURDAY EVENING, THIRTY DAYS TO THE MINUTE AFTER MY ARREST.

END

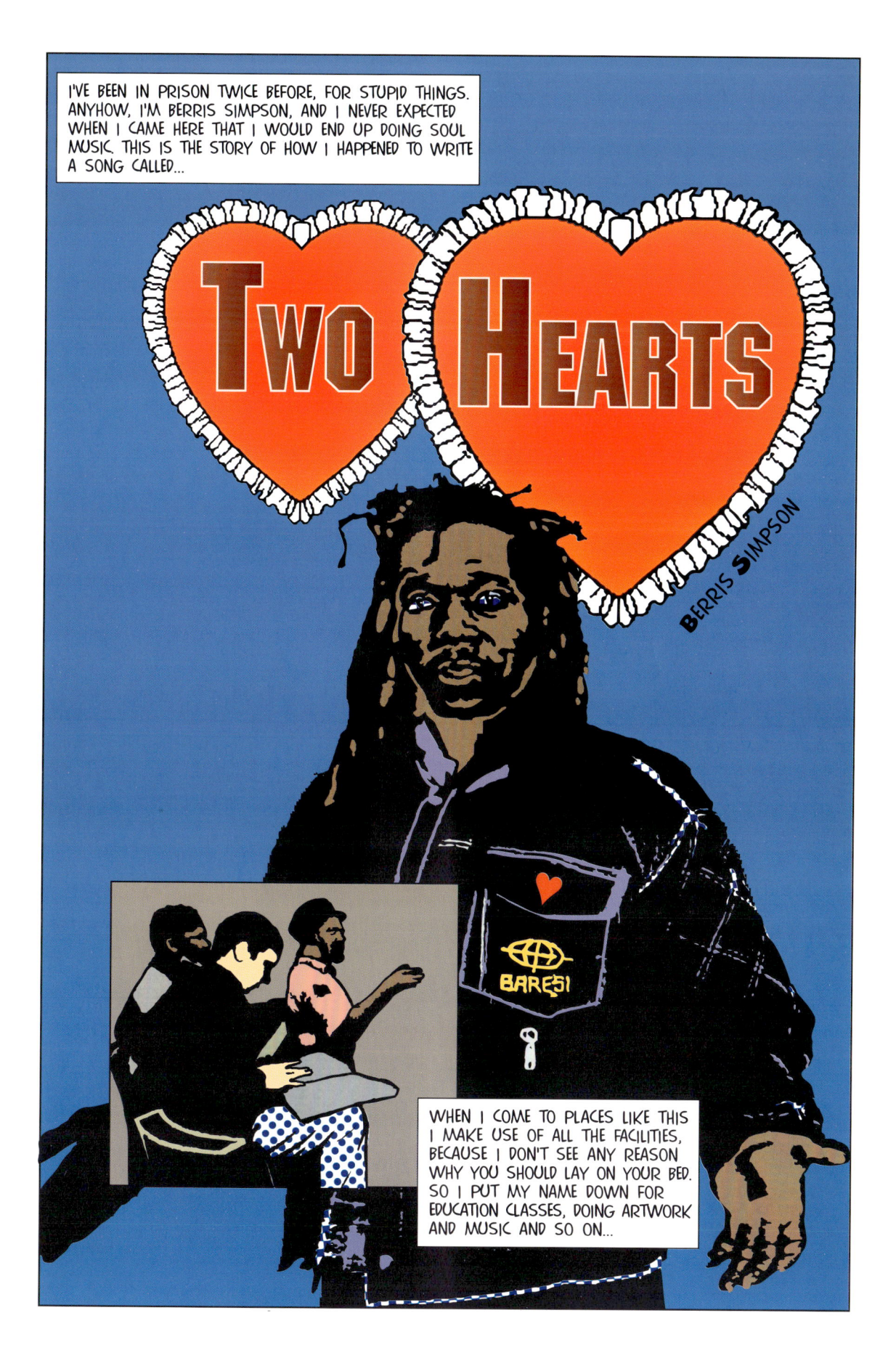

I'VE BEEN IN PRISON TWICE BEFORE, FOR STUPID THINGS. ANYHOW, I'M BERRIS SIMPSON, AND I NEVER EXPECTED WHEN I CAME HERE THAT I WOULD END UP DOING SOUL MUSIC. THIS IS THE STORY OF HOW I HAPPENED TO WRITE A SONG CALLED...

TWO HEARTS

BERRIS SIMPSON

WHEN I COME TO PLACES LIKE THIS I MAKE USE OF ALL THE FACILITIES, BECAUSE I DON'T SEE ANY REASON WHY YOU SHOULD LAY ON YOUR BED. SO I PUT MY NAME DOWN FOR EDUCATION CLASSES, DOING ARTWORK AND MUSIC AND SO ON...

SO, I STARTED ATTENDING MUSIC CLASS. I WENT DOWN ONE TIME AND I HEARD THIS MUSIC AND I JUST WENT...

WOW!

A FEW OF THE GUYS KNEW ME FROM OUTSIDE, I'M THIS GUY WHO CAN SING. I'VE BEEN AROUND BEFORE, LIKE WITH **UB40**, THE **BOOMTOWN RATS**...

I SAT DOWN AND LISTENED TO THEM, AND WHAT THEY WERE DOING WAS ALRIGHT.

WHOA! PRINCE HAMMER, THAT GUY HE KNOWS THE BUSINESS, MAN.

THERE WAS THIS GUY WHO HAD A SONG, A SOUL SORT OF THING, AND HE WAS HAVING TROUBLE ARRANGING IT, SO I WROTE IT THE WAY HE WANTED.

BUT I WANTED TO WRITE MY OWN MATERIAL FOR THE GROUP.

WHEN AM I GOING TO GET THE CHANCE TO DO A SONG MYSELF?

IN MY PAD, I CLOSED THE DOOR BEHIND ME, SO NO-ONE CAN COME UP FOR A RIZLA PAPER OR ANYTHING...

OH YES, THESE WORDS ARE OK!

ABOUT THAT TIME WE GOT ASKED TO DO A CONCERT AT THE PRISON FOR VICTIM SUPPORT.

I'LL GIVE THAT SONG I JUST WROTE. IT'S CALLED "TWO HEARTS". IT NEEDS A GIRL SINGER THOUGH.

ALL US GUYS SAT DOWN AND GOT THE BAND TOGETHER...

THEY SAID THAT THE BBC PHILHARMONIC WOULD WORK WITH US.

THIS GUY PRINCE MARLEY WROTE A SONG CALLED "DISAGREEMENT", 'CAUSE THAT'S WHAT WE WERE LIKE. I ALSO HEARD THIS WOMAN SINGING ON TAPE WITH HIM.

THAT'S EMMA. SHE HAS THE MOST BEAUTIFUL VOICE...

SHE CAN SING THE FEMALE PART ON "TWO HEARTS"

THE BIG PERFORMANCE DAY WAS COMING UP, AND WE GOT TO MEET EMMA AND THE ORCHESTRA. WE WERE IN THE GYM AND ALL OF A SUDDEN THE DOORS BURST OPEN. WE GOT TO MEET THE CONDUCTOR. IT'S ALL...

HOW ARE YOU OLD CHAP?

HERE WE GO!

(THE BBC PHILHARMONIC)

ONE TIME DURING THE REHEARSAL WE DID SOME LINES WRONG, 'CAUSE WE CAN'T READ MUSIC FROM PAPER, BUT IT WAS OK.

YO! WRONG MAN, BLAH BLAH BLAH...

AFTER REHERSAL IT WAS TIME TO GO BACK TO OUR PADS TO GET READY FOR THE CONCERT THAT NIGHT.

TWO HEARTS BEAT AS ONE...

THAT NIGHT WE WENT BACK OVER IN THE RAIN.

THOSE SCREWS ARE OUR BODYGUARD NOW. WE'RE THE STARS!

FIRST TONY AND HASSAN DID A SONG CALLED "THE SUMMIT", ABOUT DEPRIVATION, POVERTY AND STUFF. HASSAN IS REPEATING WHAT HE SAYS IN SOMALIAN.

PEACE!

I'M A MANCHESTER MAN WHO'S BEEN CUT FREE, SEVERED ROOTS FROM THE FAMILY TREE...

AGAIN!

ENCORE!

ENCORE!

NOW IT'S TIME FOR "TWO HEARTS" SUNG BY BERRIS AND EMMA! START UP THE HARP, MAN.	AND HERE COMES EMMA! EVERYBODY IS SCREAMING THEIR HEADS OFF. TWO HEARTS, BEAT AS ONE, HAS ANYONE EVER TOLD YOU ABOUT ME...
WE DO THE NUMBER REALLY ROMANTICALLY AND AT THE END....	I HAND HER A BUNCH OF FLOWERS AND GIVE HER A KISS. MORE! MORE!
WHAT CAN I SAY, IT WAS REALLY NICE. EVERYONE WENT WILD, AND WE WANTED TO STAY ALL NIGHT. YEAH! MORE!	BUT THEN ONE OF THE SCREWS SAYS... TIME TO GO BACK TO YOUR PADS, GENTLEMEN, TIME TO GO BACK TO THE PADS. END

OOP! OOP! SIMON, THIS MASK IS MY HOMAGE TO THE ART CLUB 2000.
OH! WE'RE ON! HEY, FOLKS. THOSE ARE ALL THE PRISON LIFE STORIES WE HAVE FOR YOU...
YES. WE ASKED THREE PEOPLE TO SHARE THEIR STORIES AND NOW THEY HAVE! TAKE THAT MASK OFF, DICKHEAD...
WE HAVE TO GET READY FOR OUR 'ACTION HERO' PANEL ON THE NEXT PAGE...

S & C

Since 1990, Artists Simon Grennan & Christopher Sperandio have co-created new artworks that act as bridges between diverse communities. They are progenitors of a model of the artist as a socially engaged facilitator.

Simon

Simon thrives on a diet of tea and dry toast. He lives in Manchester, England.

Chris

Chris loves coffee and eats all the wrong foods. He lives in New York City.

E. S. P.

When not sitting in airplanes, the pair are linked via modern telecommunications equipment and a singularity of purpose akin to telepathy.